We Tell It To Our Children

THE STORY OF PASSOVER

A Haggadah For Seders With Young Children

By Mary Ann Barrows Wark
Illustrated by Craig Oskow

D1710157

Mt. Zion Hebrew Congregation Rabbi's Publication Fund
and Mensch Makers Press
St. Paul, Minnesota

WE TELL IT TO OUR CHILDREN:
THE STORY OF PASSOVER
A HAGGADAH FOR SEDERS WITH
YOUNG CHILDREN

By Mary Ann Barrows Wark
Illustrations by Craig Oskow

First edition

Published by
Mt. Zion Hebrew Congregation Rabbi's Publication Fund,
1300 Summit Avenue, St. Paul, Minnesota 55105, and
Mensch Makers Press, 1588 Northrop, St. Paul, Minnesota 55108-1322

Printed in the United States of America

Library of Congress Catalog Card Number: 87-63604

ISBN 0-9619880-9-6

DEDICATION

This Haggadah is lovingly dedicated to:

The memory of my step-great-grandfather, Moses Kitzes, who gave me my first Haggadah;

The memory of my grandparents, Isedor and Rose Barrows, who celebrated traditionally; and William and Mildred Harris, who loved children;

My parents, June and Sidney Barrows, who imparted to me the love of this Jewish holiday and started our family additions to the Seder for the children and non-Jewish guests;

Dorothy Gordon and her late husband, Rabbi Albert I. Gordon, who included me in their family Seder while I was in college, and let me question how Moses did his work;

My law school friends, Alex and Fred Moses, Judith Diamond, Bev and Ralph Rivkind, who, when we each had different Haggadahs, made our Seder fun by our verbal cut-and-paste job;

My step-children, Kathleen and Jeffry Wark, who learned how important Jewish holidays are to me and who helped to make Passover a special family holiday;

My husband David M. Wark, who is my mate, my best friend, my partner in all endeavors, and a true *mensch*;

And especially my son, Barry Jay Wark, who freed me to write this to share my favorite holiday and who helped me construct our first puppets for the Seder. I am grateful to have a child who can take me places I have never been before.

MABW

To my wonderful wife, Catherine, who has helped me to realize the happiness that I've sought after, and to see things I surely would have missed.

CO

ACKNOWLEDGMENTS

With thanks to Rabbi Leigh Lerner who encouraged me from the beginning; to Rabbi Bernard Raskas who opened the doors of his congregation to try the manuscript in varying stages; to Rabbi W.Gunther Plaut, Rabbi Herbert Bronstein, and Rabbi Bruce Kadden who read the manuscript and made many helpful suggestions.

With thanks to Katherine Goldman's preschool classes and to the 6th grade class of 1984-85 at Mt. Zion Hebrew Congregation Religious School who tested my manuscript.

Thanks also to Craig Oskow who gave lots of love to this project and to his wife, Catherine Orkin Oskow, who helped me edit the manuscript.

Thanks to Steve Niedorf for his professional photographs on the back cover.

And my gratitude to my friends Barbara Shively, Mary Hess and Ardis Hutchins who listened to me, offered suggestions, and gave truly of their time; and to Barbara Shively and Julia Wark who helped me proofread.

With thanks to the Beverly Hills Chapter of Hadassah for permission to reprint the *charoset* recipes from their cookbook *From Noodles to Strudels, Volume II*, pp. 136-137. Copyright ©1980 By Beverly Hills Chapter of Hadassah.

With thanks to the Central Conference of American Rabbis for its permission to reprint the following music, lyrics, transliterations and translations from *A Passover Haggadah*, edited by Herbert Bronstein, Revised Edition: "Dayenu," "Eiliyahu Hanavi," "Ehad mi Yodeah," "Had Gadya," and "Adir Hu." Copyright ©1974 By Central Conference of American Rabbis.

Thanks to family and friends David Wark, Kathleen Wark, Jeffry Wark, Barry Wark, Sidney Barrows, Dr. William and Donna Epstein Barrows, Craig Oskow and Rochelle A. Young for modeling for various puppets and illustrations. Thanks also to June Barrows; Jack and Julia M. Wark; Michelle, Paul and Stephen Jensen; Stephen and Geoffrey Barrows; Kevin Oskow; Julie and Debra Wilensky; and Alexandra Lerner who posed for photographs.

And a special thanks to my husband and best friend, David Wark, who sat through many evenings dreaming up rhymes and thinking about how to explain this wonderful holiday to children.

TABLE OF CONTENTS

FOREWORD

The Passover Seder is the world's foremost lesson plan. It teaches the meaning of Pesach and our freedom with vivid images whose taste, sound, smell, sight and touch are remembered all through life.

Still, for the youngest of us, the Seder story is somewhat abstract. While our children are pre-schoolers and in their earliest years of elementary education, the Seder seems like a protracted adult gathering, little understood and even less participated in by the young child. Mary Ann Barrows Wark has solved this problem.

The Passover story you will create from this Haggadah is filled with action: people who have feelings, ideas that become concrete, symbols that are related to a story. Puppetry makes it live, but these puppets require no great mastery. They can be as simple as dolls or finger figures, yet children watch and listen to them eagerly.

The original Haggadah makes no mention of Moses. For our little ones, I see only benefits in telling the full tale, including Moses, who is first depicted as a helpless baby and then an ordinary person struggling to lead as God wishes. When they graduate to the classical Seder, our children will understand that we were not freed by the hands of an intermediary, but by the Holy One.

I commend this Haggadah to you. From experience I know that it is good for home use, a perfect addition to the religious school curriculum, and perhaps above all— downright fun for adults, too. You'll soon be personalizing this Haggadah, adding your own material, comments, family photos, and dances to make this service your own. It's strange and wonderful how the presence of the very young frees our imaginations and gives us permission to portray the most powerful story of Judaism with uninhibited enthusiasm.

Rabbi Leigh D. Lerner
Rabbi, Mt. Zion Hebrew Congregation
St. Paul, Minnesota
July, 1987

vii

HOW TO USE THIS HAGGADAH

This is a participatory Seder for use with small children at a family Seder, or in religious or secular school setting. You will find your 9 puppets to cut out inside the back cover of this book. I have designed this book with preparation steps and activities with the purpose of bringing the ancient and thrilling story of the Exodus to life for the smallest children and their families. There are a few preparations beyond the preparation of the ceremonial foods and the meal because I want to involve the young child in preparations and at the Seder.

PREPARATION OF THE PUPPETS

1. Finish the puppets on pages 114A-I.
• Take the puppets out of the book along the perforations. (Adult help needed.)

• Color the puppets with pencils, crayons, or markers. Add ribbons or glitter or sequins. This part of the preparation is where much learning can take place. My son and I had long discussions about which puppets were Moses' mother, sister, brother, etc. We discussed what kind of clothes they should wear because of the climate, age of the person, position in the community, wealth, etc.

• Cut out along the dotted lines.

• To make finger puppets (your second and third fingers do the walking): tape a rubber band so that it is parallel to and 1" from the bottom of the puppet. Insert your finger, so the fingers tips are feet.

                    or

• To make rod puppets: Tape the puppet to a stick (like a straw, chopstick, or pencil) or a spoon.

2. Read the story ahead of time to very young children. I urge you to read this script to your children several times before the actual Seder. Unlike adults, children enjoy the repetition — it makes the story their friend and they love to make sure it goes as they thought. In the same vein, leave the children's Haggadah on the bookshelf with the rest of your child's books for use any time during the year — remember the book is a friend.

3. Teach the songs in the month ahead. They aren't hard to learn and they tell the story of the holiday. Even non-readers will be able to participate in the Seder by singing.

PREPARATION OF THE CEREMONIAL FOODS FOR THE SEDER

These are the traditional ceremonial foods in a Seder. You may choose to prepare these a day or two ahead so that you have only the preparation of the meal for the day of the Seder. You will need a large ceremonial Seder plate to display one each of: roasted lamb bone, egg, bitter herbs, *charoset,* greens, and salt water.

Egg *(Beitzah):* A roasted egg is the symbol of an ancient festival offering as well as new life. Roast an egg for the Seder plate. For each guest, hard boil an egg and refrigerate in the shell. It is easiest to remove the shells before serving.

Greens *(karpas):* This symbol represents spring and new growth. Use parsley, watercress or celery, for Seder plate and each guest.

Bitter herb *(maror):* A radish, piece of horseradish root or prepared horseradish symbolizes the bitterness of life as slaves.

Charoset: It symbolizes mud/mortar/bricks. Jews in different parts of the world use different ingredients to get the same effect. There are several recipes included on pages 108-111. You need only prepare one variety; however, preparing more varieties gives you something exciting to taste and disuss.

Matzah: Unleavened bread made from flour and water is the most familiar Passover symbol and reminds us of the sun-baked bread made in haste on the journey from Egypt. The wheat used in the flour is carefully protected from contact with water and heat which might cause leavening. Boxes of matzah are available at Passover time in the grocery stores.

Wine and grape juice: Wine is the traditional symbol of joy. Sweet wine is traditional but many other varieties of wine are available for Passover. You will need enough for 4 cups per person.

Lamb shank bone *(Zeroah):* The lamb bone symbolizes the one used to mark the homes of Jews during the tenth plague; so that the Angel of Death would pass over. You will only need 1 for display on the Seder plate. The lamb shank bone is roasted.

Salt water: Any mixture will do to symbolize the tears of slaves.

SETTING THE TABLE TO PRESENT THE CEREMONIAL FOODS.

On the table: the traditional symbols of the Seder

    2 candles
    Wine and grape juice
    Plate with three *matzot* covered with a *matzah* cover with 3 sections
    Seder plate contains one each of: roasted egg, roasted lamb bone,
        bitter herbs (radish or horseradish), *charoset,* greens, salt water
    Elijah's cup (extra wine cup for the center of the table)
    Extra *matzah*
    Extra *charoset*
    Extra salt water

At each place: I recommend a small plate with egg, parsley, watercress or celery, *charoset,* bitter herbs and *matzah.* You could pass the ceremonial foods family style; but I prefer a small dish at each place. It allows children access to food without the disturbance of passing food.

PERFORMING THE PUPPET SHOW

Props you need to get: 1 doll for Baby Moses and a basket to put it in, and *afikomen* (hidden middle matzah) rewards - traditionally money.

Assign the roles before you begin reading this at Seder. At our house, we assign roles before we sit down so that the story starts quickly for the children once everyone is seated. In general, reading adults will have to operate the puppets, with the exception of the sheep. The four-year-old children at our Seder have tried to work the puppets while the adult did the voice (and reading). There are 10 parts and 5 scenes. Scene 5 requires 6 puppets, but the rest do not require that many. *All stage directions are in italics.*

Character	Scene	Level of reading needed
Moses (baby)	Introd., 2	
Moses (adult)	3,4,5	
Aaron, Moses' brother	5	beginner can handle
Miriam, Moses' sister	2,5,	
Yocheved, Moses' mom	2	
Pharaoh	1,5	
Princess	2	
Slave	1,3,5	
Sheep	4	non-reader can handle
Taskmaster	3,5	
Narrator	1,2,3,4,5	

Performing time:
Approximately 45 minutes. Don't let the time scare you— the two-year-olds at our family Seder and the three-year-old classroom for whom we regularly do this show sit easily— asking many questions along the way.

To add more roles: Add more sheep, goats, or other cattle.

HOW IS THIS HAGGADAH DIFFERENT FROM THE OTHER 29,000 PUBLISHED HAGGADAHS?

This Haggadah has several special features:

1. You will tell the story in the dramatic voice rather than in the narrative voice. Small children will stay interested because they can follow the character changes. The adults will have fun making the story come to life. The puppets are the added "guests" and the story has a "you-are-there" quality.

2. The order of the service is changed; so that the ceremonial food symbols appear when the story explains them. Seder means "order;" so the change is a real one.

The order in the traditional Haggadah is:
    Blessing over the wine— first cup
    Hand washing
    Karpas dipped in salt water
    Breaking the middle matzah
    Four Questions
    Reading from the Haggadah
    Dayenu
    Discussion of the symbolic foods
    Second cup of wine
    Hand washing
    Blessing of the matzah
    Maror dipped in charoset
    Hillel sandwich (matzah and bitter herbs)
    Meal
    In Ashkenazi homes, afikomen
    Grace after the meal
    Third cup of wine
    Open the door for Elijah
    Praises of God
    Fourth cup of wine
    Songs after the meal

Why did I change the order? Because I wanted to integrate the symbols with the story. In this Haggadah, the Four Questions are optional because the children in attendance may be very young. Because the whole rationale for this Haggadah is to tell the story for "the child who is yet unable to inquire," the traditional Four Sons are omitted. Almost all the ceremony precedes the meal to accommodate toddlers and preschoolers. Thus, I put the 3rd cup of wine and opening the door for Elijah before the meal because once the children are paying attention, I wanted them to get as much of the Seder as possible. If your family would like to look forward to the opening of the door for Elijah after the meal, I have noted in the text where to insert it.

3. Non-readers can fully participate from the beginning to the end of the Seder, as well as join in the traditional ways of asking the Four Questions, searching for the *afikomen* and watching Elijah's cup. By learning four simple song parodies, they can help tell the story also. Even two-year-olds easily learn the refrains. Preschoolers are able to handle the non-speaking animal puppets. New readers are able to handle Aaron's role.

4. I have added song parodies based on American folk songs because the melodies are familiar to all with young children, and you will have no trouble singing them easily the first time around. "It Made Them Mad" and "Bad Things Will Come To Egypt (The Plagues)" alone tell the story and can be sung on their own. However, the traditional melodies are ones that help us have common customs, and if you know the songs, we encourage you to sing them at the traditional time, after the meal. Some favorite traditional songs are included on pages 102-6.

5. There is a special section for family photos on pages 2 and 3 and on page 112, a place to enter names of guests who played the puppet roles to make this your own family's Haggadah. My further purpose in including these pages is to begin to teach our children about world Jewry by starting with our own family.

6. Passover is celebrated with cultural variations, and I have tried to incorporate some of them. You will find recipes for *charoset* which add variety to our family Seder and make us think of the other parts of the world where Jews celebrate. The *afikomen* tradition is Askenazi; placing the *matzah* in the napkin and walking around the table is Sephardic.

7. This book is designed to be folded back while holding the book in one hand and the puppet in the other. As the reader folds the book back, the pictures are on the back side and visible to the children around the table. The pictures each have a caption; so that the Haggadah can be used as a picture book in preparation for the holiday or by the non-reading child in solitude. The pictures alone tell the story.

8. Without knowing Hebrew, you can fully present all the blessings because they appear in Hebrew, transliteration of the Hebrew, and English translation. The blessings are set in a different typestyle so that they are easy to find during the Seder. In a secular setting, they can be omitted. If you don't know the Hebrew and find the transliterations difficult, the English translation gives the meaning of the blessing.

DO WE INFANTALIZE THE PASSOVER TRADITIONS BY SETTING THEM IN THE DRAMATIC VOICE, ADDING HUMOR AND SONG?

I believe I have faithfully retold the story in all its detail and drama. This is not a watered-down and sanitized version. I have raised many questions over the years: Did Moses know he was Jewish when he was in the palace? How did he know? Did others in the palace know? How did he feel when there were anti-Jewish discussions? How did Moses persuade his own people to go along with him? How did he deal with Pharaoh? What was it like when the plagues came? How did they affect Egyptians? Jews? I tried to pose answers to some of these questions. I hope you will raise and try to answer questions too. The true celebration of this holiday of freedom requires each participant to feel the issues, to grapple with the inherent dilemmas, and hopefully to forge a part of the self to deal with the issues as they are real in our lives.

Many Haggadahs add sections to deal with the current struggles for freedom. I believe that very young children need to understand that the world is bigger than their own family and have included pages at the beginning for you to expand the young child's Jewish world. I encourage you to add sections on the current struggles for freedom with the 4th cup of wine on page 95.

HOW MANY CHILDREN DO YOU NEED TO PERFORM THIS?

If you have 25 adults and 1 child, should you choose to use this Haggadah? We are commanded to tell the story in its entirety. I believe it is easier when there is a purpose--telling it so that everyone can really understand it. Whether you tell the story for a child or a non-Jewish person, or for a different view of the story for yourself, I believe that having this purpose will help you be a better, more complete storyteller. I believe it is just as interesting to perform for the adults as it is for the children. If you use a traditional Haggadah for the first Seder, why not choose this one for the second Seder?

IF YOU USE THIS WHEN YOUR CHILDREN ARE SMALL, WHEN DO YOU USE A TRADITIONAL HAGGADAH?

I intend this Haggadah for use with children ages 2-12. Those who are non-readers can be animal characters and can sing the songs. Those who are beginning readers will find it fun to be a character with easy lines. I tried to use a simplified (but colorful) vocabulary.

MODEL SEDERS OR CLASSROOM USE

Many Christians have model seders to learn about Jesus' Last Supper. This Haggadah is fun and appropriate for adults at a model Seder. The perspective is authentically Jewish.

You can easily adapt this script for **classroom** use. You could add a puppet stage, and sets or scenery such as Pharaoh's palace; the work site; by the bullrushes; the wilderness; by the shores of the Red Sea.

More elaborate hand puppets could be constructed. For our own family we constructed soft sculpture puppets for the human characters and mouth puppets for the animals. There are wonderful how-to puppet books available in libraries and bookstores. You may want to construct a narrator puppet.

Older elementary children can perform for younger children. Parents also can perform for young children in a classroom.

The blessings are set in a different typestyle which allows you to omit them in a secular setting.

INEVITABLE SPILLS

It is hard to make Seders with young children formal affairs. So too, it is likely that someone, child or grown up will spill. At our house, we tell everyone the salt is to heap on spilled wine or grape juice. We announce that if someone spills, no one will get angry. A drop or two on this Haggadah will make it part of the family.

We hope you enjoy your holiday as much as we do at our house.

Mary Ann Barrows Wark
St. Paul, Minnesota
1987

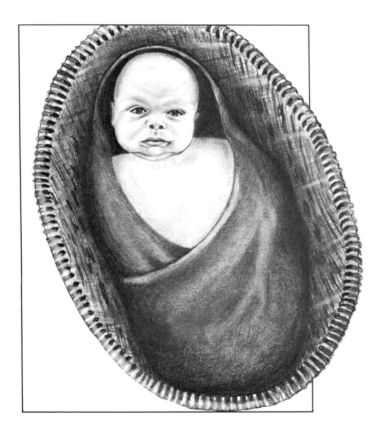

"There, there, stop crying my little Moses."

WE TELL IT TO OUR CHILDREN: THE STORY OF PASSOVER
INTRODUCTION

Narrator: *(With doll as baby Moses in arms)* There, there, stop crying my little Moses. I know there are lots of people here. You know we were going to tell them a story about you.

We are so glad everyone here could join our family for this Seder, our special meal to celebrate the beginning of Passover. You know, Moses, we are here with people we love and we have all these special, delicious-smelling foods and things in front of us at our table. Wouldn't it make us happy if we could share this Seder with anyone who is hungry or thirsty? Are you hungry and thirsty? Then you may have some, too. We are lucky tonight, Moses, because we are free. We would like all who need love, food or drink to come share our meal and the hope that Passover tells us about.

Do you know that tonight we think about people in our family who can not be here with us tonight, and in that way, we join with our people everywhere? Would you like to see the pictures?

[Insert picture of the family at whose house the Seder is.]

[Insert pictures of members of the family who can't be with you.]

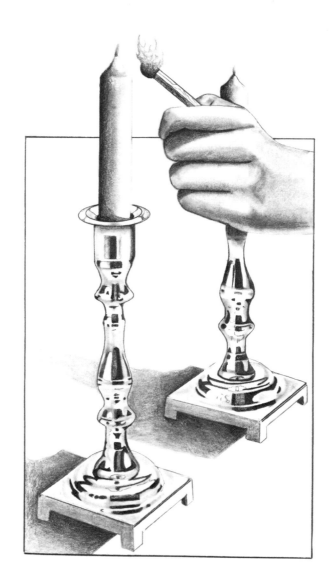

We light the candles on special days.

Narrator: But you are not in the story in the beginning. Do you think you would be able to sleep in your basket until we tell the part of the story about you? We'll try to be quiet, and we might even sing you some songs. I'll tell you what we'll do—

Narrator: When it is time to tell about you, we'll have the kids wake you up. *[To kids]* Will you help me when I tell you? We'll say gently, "Moses, it's time." OK? OK. *[Put doll (baby Moses) in the basket near the table.]* Now shhhh...go to sleep.

LIGHTING THE CANDLES

Narrator: We light the candles on the special days when we are together. Tonight we think about coming out of the darkness of slavery into the light of freedom. Thank you God that we are free tonight and can share the warm feelings of our families and friends.

All: בָּרוּךְ אַתָּה יְיָ אֱלֹהֵינוּ מֶלֶךְ הָעוֹלָם אֲשֶׁר קִדְּשָׁנוּ בְּמִצְוֹתָיו וְצִוָּנוּ לְהַדְלִיק נֵר שֶׁל (שַׁבָּת וְשֶׁל) יוֹם טוֹב.

Baruch Atah Adonai, Eloheinu Melech ha'olam, asher kidshanu bemitzvotav vetzivanu lehadlik ner shel (shabbat v'shel) Yom Tov.

We praise You, O Lord our God, Ruler of the Universe, who has commanded us to kindle the lights of (the Sabbath and) this festival.

בָּרוּךְ אַתָּה יְיָ אֱלֹהֵינוּ מֶלֶךְ הָעוֹלָם שֶׁהֶחֱיָנוּ וְקִיְּמָנוּ וְהִגִּיעָנוּ לַזְּמַן הַזֶּה.

Baruch Atah Adonai, Eloheinu Melech ha'olam, shehecheyanu vekimanu vehigianu lazman hazeh.

We praise You, O Lord our God, Ruler of the Universe, who has given us life, kept us alive and brought us to this happy occasion.

OPTIONAL FOUR QUESTIONS

[If there is a child who is able to recite, you may insert the traditional Four Questions here or at the end at page 96.]

Narrator: Do we have someone who would like the honor of reciting the Four Questions?

Child: מַה נִּשְׁתַּנָּה הַלַּיְלָה הַזֶּה מִכָּל הַלֵּילוֹת.

Ma nish-ta-na ha-lei-lah ha-zeh mi-kol ha-lei lot?

Why is this night different from all other nights?

שֶׁבְּכָל הַלֵּילוֹת אָנוּ אוֹכְלִין חָמֵץ וּמַצָּה, הַלַּיְלָה הַזֶּה כֻּלּוֹ מַצָּה.

She-b'-hol ha-lei-lot a-nu oh-lin-ha'metz u-matzah. Ha-lai-lah ha-zeh, ku-lo ma-tzah.

On all other nights, we eat either leavened bread or matzah; on this night—only matzah.

שֶׁבְּכָל הַלֵּילוֹת אָנוּ אוֹכְלִין שְׁאָר יְרָקוֹת, הַלַּיְלָה הַזֶּה מָרוֹר.

She-b'-hol ha-lei lot a-nu oh-lin sh'-ar y'-ra kot. Ha-lei-lah ha-zeh, maror.

On all other nights, we eat all kinds of herbs; on this night, we especially eat bitter herbs.

שֶׁבְּכָל הַלֵּילוֹת אֵין אָנוּ מַטְבִּילִין אֲפִילוּ פַּעַם אֶחָת, הַלַּיְלָה הַזֶּה שְׁתֵּי פְעָמִים.

She-be-hol ha-lei-lot ein a-nu mat-bi-lin a-fi-lu pa-am e-hat. Ha-lai-lah ha-zeh, sh-tai-pi-ah-mim.

On all other nights, we do not dip herbs at all; on this night we dip them twice.

6

שֶׁבְּכָל הַלֵּילוֹת אָנוּ אוֹכְלִין בֵּין יוֹשְׁבִין וּבֵין מְסֻבִּין, הַלַּיְלָה הַזֶּה כֻּלָּנוּ מְסֻבִּין.

She-bi-hul ha-lei-lot a-nu och-lin bein yosh-vin oo-vein mis-oo-been. Ha-lai-lah ha-zeh, ku-la-nu m'-su-bin.

On all other nights, we eat in an ordinary manner; tonight we dine with special ceremony.

Narrator: And now, let's tell the story of Passover.
This is our cast— the other people who are joining us tonight to tell the story. Help me welcome them by clapping as they each take a bow.
[The person holding the puppet of each character should make that character ''bow'' as his/her name is read]

Moses
Aaron
Miriam
Yocheved
Pharaoh
Princess
Slave
Sheep
Taskmaster
Narrator

(These are the props: doll and basket.)

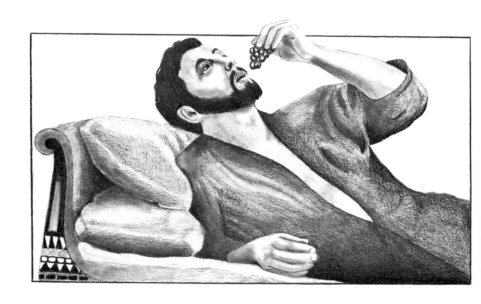

Rich or well-off people sat or lay down on pillows to eat.

Narrator: Once upon a time, really a very long time ago, there was a man named Jacob. He was a Jew, and he lived with his family far away, in a place called Israel, that would take us many, many hours to get to from here if we flew very fast in a plane.

Now there was also a man who was the king of Egypt. The Egyptians called all their kings Pharaoh, and this one was called Pharaoh, too. Egypt was not too far from Israel but it would take several weeks to walk there from Israel. You know, they did not have cars or trains or buses or airplanes in those days.

When Pharaoh needed help doing something, he tried to get the best person to help him. One time, he asked one of Jacob's sons, a man named Joseph, to help him. Joseph saved lots and lots of people from starving in Egypt. He was such a big help that the king, Pharaoh, decided that he would do something nice for Joseph. What do you think would be something nice to do for someone who had saved the lives of lots of your people? *[Give people a chance to answer— it helps make this their story, too.]*

Well, this nice Pharaoh really appreciated the help, and he decided that he would give Joseph a good job, and he also would let all of Joseph's family come to Egypt and live well, too. Joseph's whole family, including old Jacob, came to live in Egypt with Joseph. In the beginning it seemed that living in Egypt was very different from where they had come from, but soon they were very happy living there.

RECLINING ON PILLOWS

Narrator: You notice how comfortably we sit here tonight. In ancient times, people who were rich or well-off sat or lay down on pillows to eat.

9

Grapes

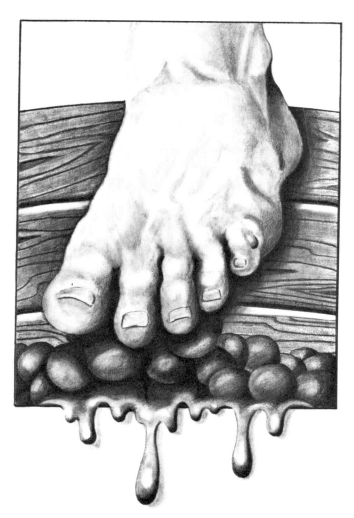

Stomping on grapes to get the juice out

THE FIRST CUP OF WINE

Narrator: They also had a drink that came from the juice of grapes. The grapes grew outside in the place where the Jews used to live. It took lots of grapes to make enough juice for just one cup of wine.

Taste the sweet wine or grape juice.

Narrator: A special kind of joy came from people's work of freeing the good sweet juice from inside the fruit. They were happy that they had wine to drink and they thanked God for it. We, too, thank God for this special fruit, for this special drink, for this special day, and for these special people to share our joy as the Jews must have long ago.

Let's sing the kiddush together:

All: בָּרוּךְ אַתָּה יְיָ אֱלֹהֵינוּ מֶלֶךְ הָעוֹלָם בּוֹרֵא פְּרִי הַגָּפֶן.

Baruch Atah Adonai, Eloheinu Melech ha'olam, borei peri hagafen.

We praise You, Oh God, Ruler of the Universe, Who creates the fruit of the vine.

Narrator: Now we may taste the sweet wine.

All: *[Drink first cup of wine.]*

13

Pharaoh

14

Narrator: Many years passed. Joseph's father, Jacob, died. Joseph died, and so did his brothers. Even the good king, Pharaoh, died. Of course, by then there were a lot more of Joseph's family in Egypt, because a lot of his children had been born and had grown up and had had children of their own. There was a new Pharaoh, and that is where some of the problem started. Because this Pharaoh was mean.

Pharaoh: *[Show puppet of Pharaoh]*

All: **Hiss**

Scene 1

In which we find out what it is like to live when the new Pharaoh is king.

(Pharaoh, Slave, Narrator)

Pharaoh: There are a lot of Jews in my country now. What kind of people are they? They came from some other place—they are not really Egyptian and I don't trust any of them. What if there were a war some day? They may turn out to be an enemy and fight against the Egyptians! I've got to figure out something so they won't ever cause me any trouble. I've got it! I'll tell them that they have to work for me! At first I'll pay them, but then I'll stop even paying them. Then they will be real slaves, and they'll never be able to hurt Egypt. I'll have them make bricks out of mud and straw and then take the bricks to make walls all around my biggest cities—that'll keep them busy for years. I'll have the grandest cities around, and the Jews won't have time or energy to be against me. They won't have any time to make more children; and I hope some of them will die so there won't be so many of them.

15

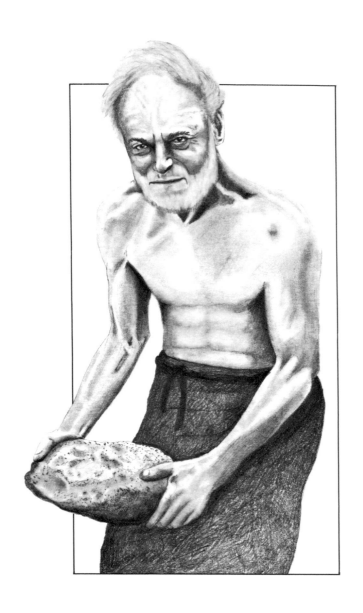

Slave

Slave: I am forced to work very hard for Pharaoh now. I can't raise my crops or my sheep anymore. I don't get much chance to be with my family either— and I hardly ever get any rest. I don't have so much to eat any more because I don't have time to work in the fields to raise my crops. And that isn't the worst of it—if I don't work hard enough, the Egyptians beat me and hurt me. They might even kill me. I want to keep on living— so, I keep working.

All:

Song: "I've Been Working on These Buildings"
(To the tune of: "I've Been Working on the Railroad")

I've been working on these buildings;
Pharaoh doesn't pay.
I've been doing what he tells me
Like making bricks from clay.
Can't you hear the master calling,
"Hurry up, make a brick!"
Can't you see the master hurt me
Until I'm feeling sick.
Oh is this a mess,
Oh is this a mess,
Oh is this a mess for Jews, for Jews.
Oh is this a mess,
Oh is this a mess,
Oh is this a mess for Jews.
Someone's in the palace with Pharaoh —
Someone's in the palace we know,ow,ow,ow,
Someone's in the palace with Pharaoh —
Does he know they treat us so?
Keep singing work, work, work all day,
Work all day and then some mo–ore,
Work, work, work all day —
Does he know they treat us so?

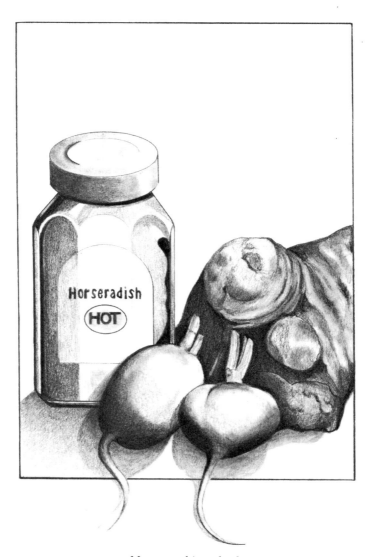

Maror or bitter herbs

MAROR OR BITTER HERBS

Narrator: Do you see or smell something on your plate that you think might taste bitter and not sweet? *[Show bitter herb on Seder plate—radish or horseradish]*. Tonight we eat bitter herbs like the radish or horseradish on our plates because Pharaoh treated us meanly as slaves in Egypt. That unkind way of treating us made us feel awful. We say that it was a bitter time, and we eat bitter herbs to remind us how bitter it was. If even a little bit of something bitter makes us feel bad, imagine how terrible and nasty it must have been for the Jews all of the time in Egypt.

Even for food that is bitter, though, we are thankful to God, so please join me in the blessing.

All: בָּרוּךְ אַתָּה יְיָ אֱלֹהֵינוּ מֶלֶךְ הָעוֹלָם אֲשֶׁר קִדְּשָׁנוּ בְּמִצְוֹתָיו וְצִוָּנוּ עַל אֲכִילַת מָרוֹר.

Baruch Atah Adonai, Eloheinu Melech ha'olam, asher kideshanu bemitzvotav vetzivanu al achilat maror.

We praise You, O Lord our God, Ruler of the Universe, Who makes our lives holy through commandments, who has commanded us to remember how bad it feels to be slaves by eating bitter herbs.

Charoset

CHAROSET

Narrator: Now can you find something on your plates that reminds you of mud or clay for bricks or for the mortar in between them? *[Point out charoset.]*

We eat *charoset* to remind us how the Jews had to make bricks for Pharaoh. No one paid for our work, and it was hard work that we didn't want to do. We can also eat *charoset* and *maror* together since making the bricks caused bitterness. Another way to try eating it is with *matzah,* and then we call it a Hillel sandwich.

All: *[Eat charoset.]*

"This calls for a new plan."

Narrator: Even as slaves, the Jews did have more and more children, until it seemed to Pharaoh that the Jews from Jacob and Joseph's family were everywhere, and were most of the people in Egypt. They did a lot of work for Pharaoh too.

Pharaoh: Everything has gone just as I planned to keep the Jews here, but harmless. It has turned out to be a great system for getting my big palaces and cities built cheaply. But it might not have been so smart of me, after all, because now someone has warned me that a Jewish boy will be born who will lead his people out of Egypt. The problem is that the person could not tell me which boy it will be. Whom would I have to do my work if the Jews left Egypt? And maybe they'd fight Egypt if they left, and they'd have more men than we do. This calls for a new plan. Hmmmmm. How about this? Every newborn Jewish baby boy will be thrown into the river and drowned. If there are no Jewish baby boys—then there can be no Jewish baby boy who can grow up and lead the Jewish people out of Egypt. Right?

All: Hiss.

Pharaoh: You must be on their side. Well, I'm the King and that is the way I'm going to do it.

Narrator: The Egyptians kept track of pregnant women, so they could tell when each baby was going to be born. Then they would go to the mother about the time she was going to have a baby. If it were a baby boy, they would take the little boy away from his mother and just throw him into the river. How do you think the mothers felt about losing their newborn babies? You know of course, the baby would drown because babies can't swim. But one Jewish boy was saved— and this is how it happened.

"Now I have an idea. I am going to hide him."

SCENE 2

In which we find out how one Jewish baby boy was saved
(**Narrator/Baby Moses, Yocheved, Miriam, Princess**)

Narrator: In Egypt lived a Jewish woman named Yocheved and her husband, Amram. They had two children already, Aaron and Miriam. Yocheved was going to have a baby, after the Pharaoh made up his new plan. Now kids, do you think we could gently wake up little Moses. I'm sure he'll want to hear this part of the story because it is about when he was born. Let's all say: "Moses, now the story is about you. Wake up!"

All: **Moses, now the story is about you. Wake up!**

Narrator: We'll just give him to his real mother now. Here he is Yocheved. *[Give doll as baby Moses to Yocheved.]*

Yocheved: This is my baby boy. *[Hold up doll.]* He was just born today. Isn't he handsome? He was born three months earlier than I expected. He is so very little. I should be very happy to have a baby. But the Egyptians drown all the baby boys, and you know it would break my heart if he were taken from me. For months I have been trying to find a way to keep him. Now I have an idea. I am going to hide him. They can't even suspect that I have him for three months yet.

Narrator: Those three months went by very quickly for Yocheved and her baby boy, who was growing nicely.

Miriam watched Moses in the bulrush plants along the river.

Yocheved: The Egyptians will come for my baby boy any day now. But I finally have a plan I think will work. I am making a tiny boat out of the reeds that grow by the river. See this basket? I'm putting mud and tar on the outside so it will keep out the water. There, it's done. *[Put doll in basket.]* Now isn't that cozy, my baby boy? Now I'll just hide you in the bulrush plants along the edge of the river. *[Put basket and doll near some close plant like the center piece.]*

Miriam, my daughter, you stay and watch what happens to your baby brother. I'll go back home until the Egyptians come, and I'll just tell them the baby died already. Oh, I'll cry and tell them how sad I am so they believe me. Miriam, you hide until you see what happens to him. If some Egyptians rescue him— that's what I hope will happen— ask if they need a woman to nurse him— then come to get me quickly. Now be sure to watch, and don't fall asleep.

Miriam: I hope she's right because it's all hot and buggy sitting here in these weeds. I hope someone comes soon.

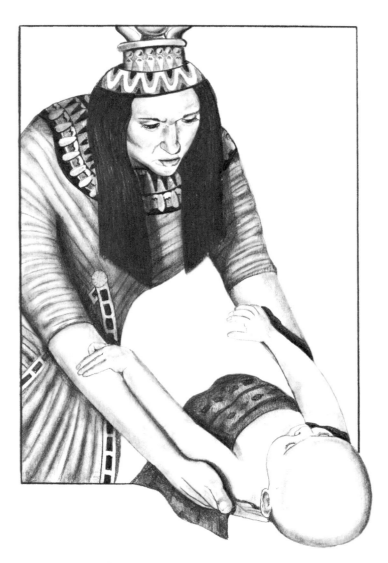

An Egyptian Princess found Moses.

Princess: I am an Egyptian Princess. I should be happy, they say, because I am rich and have everything I want. But I don't have what I really want—a baby.

Oh my goodness. Look what I've found in the river. *[Takes basket out of the river.]* A baby. *[Make baby noises at the baby.]* And it's a boy, too. This will be my baby boy. I will call him "Moses", because I took him from the water, and I will take him to the palace to live with me. I don't know who he is, but he will be raised like a prince as my son.

Miriam: Hello.

Princess: Hello. Look what I've just found, a poor little baby boy. Oh, no, he's crying. He must be hungry, because he isn't wet or cold. Now what am I going to do?

Miriam: Maybe you need someone to nurse your baby.

Princess: Sure, that's just what I need, because this baby is so young, he can't eat regular food yet. I hope I can find someone who can nurse him.

Miriam: I know someone who would be the perfect nurse for your baby. Do you want me to get her?

Princess: Oh, yes. *[Nod head.]*

Miriam: I'll go to get her then. Her name is Yocheved. *[Go to Yocheved]*

[Excited] Mom, an Egyptian princess has Moses and she wants you to come right away to nurse him. He's crying because he's hungry, but— he's OK.

Moses knew the Princess loved him, but he knew his people lived beyond the palace walls.

Yocheved: God has heard my prayers. My boy will live and I can be with him for a while yet. But who would have imagined a princess would save him! I'd hoped some Egyptian would save him— but the Princess, whose very own father wants to have all the Jewish baby boys killed? Oh, my goodness, if Pharaoh only knew. Is it too much to hope, dear God, that the Princess will really love my son as I would?

SCENE 3

In which Moses hurts an Egyptian
(Narrator, Taskmaster, Slave, Moses)

Narrator: Well, the Princess did just that—she raised him with love, as her son, the Prince. As Moses grew older, he knew he was a Jew, even though he was living in the Egyptian palace and no one there, except the Princess, knew. It was hard for him to live like a prince and hear that his people suffered as slaves. He heard Egyptians in the palace say horrible things about Jews. He hated that, but he was lucky the Princess loved him and would not tell anyone else in the palace that he was Jewish. He wanted to see for himself, though, how his people were treated. One day he left the palace, which Princes never did, and went to where the Jewish slaves were working.

Taskmasters were cruel to the workers.

Taskmaster: You didn't work hard enough. Take this. *[Beat up.]*

Slave: Don't hit me. Can't you see I'm working as hard as I can?

Moses: Don't hit him. How can you treat him like that? He is weak from all the work he does for you. If you don't stop that, I will show you how it feels. *[Beat up taskmaster, Punch and Judy style.]*

Taskmaster: Aggggggh! *[Fall over, "dead."]*

33

"Oh, no! What have I done?"

Moses: Oh no, what have I done? *[Cry]* I didn't mean to kill the Egyptian. If Pharaoh ever finds out, he will have me killed, too. I know that's the law— even if I am a prince. I'm going to have to leave Egypt and find somewhere else to live. I'll be sad to leave the Princess, who has been so good to me. But even she won't be able to help me now. I must leave. That's the only choice I have if I want to live.

"Living in a tent is so different from living in a palace."

SCENE 4
In which Moses is a shepherd
(Moses, sheep, Narrator)

Narrator: Moses ran a long way away, to a place called Midian. It was hard to leave his home, but after a while the sadness left. He married a woman there named Zipporah, and he took care of sheep for her father. He never forgot Egypt, though.

Moses: Oh, it is so peaceful here watching the sheep.

Sheep: Baa, baa.

Moses: Living in a tent is so different from living in a palace. I'm proud of myself that I've learned to find food and water for these sheep in this wilderness where it isn't easy to find something for the animals to eat or drink. Everything is so beautiful that I'm beginning to think that maybe my sister Miriam was right when she told me there was a God.

Sheep: Baa,baa.

" Who Me?"

Moses: What do I see? I've never seen anything like that before! A bush that has fire in it but is not all burned up. How is it staying alive and green? Now I'm scared.

Narrator: Then Moses heard a small voice calling to him, but there was no person around. The voice was coming from inside the burning bush. "Moses,Moses."

Moses: Here I am.

Narrator: It was God speaking to Moses. "I have heard the crying of my people. I will get them out of Egypt, but you must be their first leader."

Moses: Me? You must be kidding! I can't be their leader. How can I be their leader? If I go back to Egypt, they'll kill me. I'm no good at speaking either. No one would listen if I speak.

Narrator: God told Moses to get his older brother, Aaron, who was a good speaker, to do the talking. And besides, the old Pharaoh, who used to be there when Moses killed the Egyptian, was gone.

Moses: What if the people won't believe me or don't believe You sent me? Hey, I'm not even sure I believe You.

Narrator: God did some spectacular things right there in front of Moses' eyes. God turned Moses' shepherd's stick into a snake— and then back into a stick again! God told Moses to put his hand inside his robe, and take it out again. When Moses took his hand out, it looked like the skin was all sick! Then God told Moses to put his hand inside his robe and take it out again. This time the skin looked all healthy! And God promised to do the same thing in front of the Jews. It was quiet again. Very quiet.

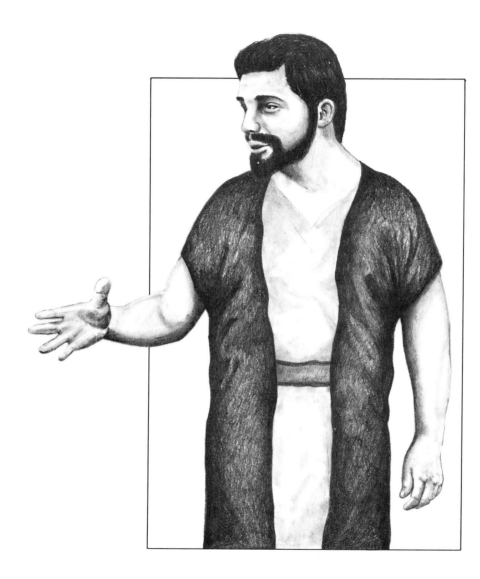

Aaron was already a leader.

Sheep: Baa, baa.

Narrator: What a job God had asked Moses to do! Where would he start? First of all, he would have to leave Midian; and that would be hard because he loved his wife's family so much. But they loved him too, and they had always thought that he would go back to Egypt some day, even though he had never believed it. He left Midian with his wife and his two children.

Second, Moses would have to find his brother Aaron. Luckily, he had no trouble finding Aaron, who was already a leader of his people in Egypt.

Then Moses convinced Aaron and the people that God wanted him to help them. It was hard to get people who were used to being slaves and scared of the Egyptians to believe in the possibility of freedom. They were not going to hurt the Egyptians, but they all agreed that Moses should go to Pharaoh and convince him to let them go.

All:

Song: "Let My People Go" (or "Go Down Moses")

When Israel was in Egypt land
Let my People go
Oppressed so hard they could not stand
Let my People go.
Go down, Moses
Way down in Egypt land
Tell old Pharaoh
To let my People go.

Moses was ready to go to Pharaoh.

SCENE 5

In which Moses and Aaron ask Pharaoh to let the Jews leave Egypt

(Moses, Aaron, Pharaoh, Miriam, Slave, Taskmaster, Narrator)

Narrator: The Jews were working harder than ever, and Moses and Aaron talked with them about God's plan. They weren't sure how long it would take, but they knew they had to try. So Moses and Aaron went to Pharaoh on one of those days when the Pharaoh would listen to the problems of any person. Convincing Pharaoh—that was going to be the hardest part, a lot harder than convincing the Jews.

Karpas or greens dipped in salt water

KARPAS (GREENS) DIPPED
IN SALT WATER

Narrator: Just as the Jews then had to wait a long time to get away from Pharaoh, we have to wait a long time for spring during a long winter. It may still be wintery outside, but the parsley on our plates is green, and it lets us think that spring will soon be here, and things will again be green outside.

It was not fun waiting in Egypt then. Because the Jews were frustrated, angry and sad, they cried salty tears many times before they were free, and while they were waiting to leave Egypt. So tonight we will dip our parsley into salt water, so that we, too, will taste the salt water of tears with the parsley of hope.

All: בָּרוּךְ אַתָּה יְיָ אֱלֹהֵינוּ מֶלֶךְ הָעוֹלָם בּוֹרֵא פְּרִי הָאֲדָמָה.

Baruch Atah Adonai, Eloheinu Melech ha'olam, borei peri ha'adamah.

Praised are You, Oh Lord, Our God, Ruler of the Universe, who creates the fruit of the earth.

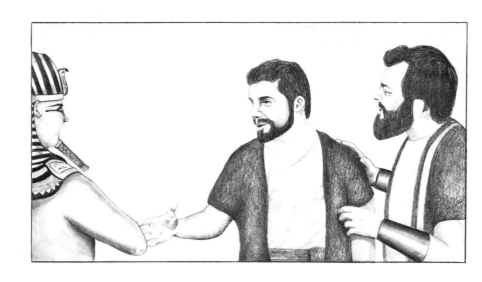

Aaron and Moses going to Pharaoh

Moses: Aaron, don't even ask him at first to let us totally leave Egypt. Just ask if he'll let us go pray to God.

Aaron: Pharaoh, please let us Jews pray to God in the desert. It would take us about three days to get to the place we need to go.

Pharaoh: No slaves ever come here and aren't scared. How dare you? And slaves don't get vacations either. If I give a vacation to the Jews, all the other kinds of slaves will want one too. No. What a crazy excuse—who is this God?

Moses: *[To Aaron]* We'd better leave the palace now. We'll have to come back some other time.

Pharaoh: Increase their work load. They still have to make as many bricks, but now we won't give them the straw to make them. That should teach them to remember they're slaves and I'm the boss. It will also make them angry at these two slaves Moses and Aaron. That couldn't hurt.

Slave: The Pharaoh is making us work harder than ever. I didn't think that was possible. If our God knows we suffer, why has God asked us to do something even harder? Are you sure this is going to work? Sometimes I'm not so sure.

Moses: I never believed he'd agree on the first try. We'll just have to go to Pharaoh again. We've got to be free the way we used to be; so we must keep on trying. And remember, God promised to help.

"No, no, no, no!"

All:

> **Song: "It Made them Mad"**
> *(To the tune of: "Clementine")*
>
> **It made them mad to hear the answer**
> **Pharaoh would not let them go.**
> **God would help them with a signal.**
> **Mighty power God would show.**
>
> **No, no, no, no, no, no, no, no,**
> **That was all that Pharaoh said.**
> **With no way to beat his army,**
> **They would change his mind instead.**

Moses: This time, Aaron, we'll have to ask him just to let us go, plain and simple.

Aaron: Please let my people leave Egypt, Pharaoh.

Pharaoh: No, why should I? I need my slaves.

Moses: Our God says to.

Pharaoh: Your God, eh. Well that just about takes the cake. Listen here, you slave, I pick the gods around here and I've picked the good ones. Why should I listen to the God of slaves?

Instead of water, there was blood.

All:
Song: " Plagues" verse 1 (Blood)
(To the tune of: "She'll Be Coming 'Round the Mountain")

Bad things will come to Egypt,don't you know
Bad things will come to Egypt,don't you know
Bad things will come to Egypt,
Bad things will come to Egypt,
Bad things will come to Egypt till we go.

First, God will change the water into blood
    (ick, ick)
First, God will change the water into blood
    (ick, ick)
There'll be nothing left to drink;
With no baths you all will stink
When God changes all the water into blood.
    (ick, ick)

Narrator: Imagine where water is. Can you name a few places where it is? *[Give them a chance to answer.]* That's right: in the lakes, in the oceans, in the rivers, in cups, in jars. All the water, everywhere, turned to blood. No one had anything to drink. They were all scared. Pharaoh almost let them go... But then the blood finally became water again, and he changed his mind. Moses went back to Pharaoh after everything was all right again.

Moses: Aaron, tell Pharaoh that our God has shown Pharaoh that God is a powerful God, and Pharaoh had better listen to us and let us go.

Aaron: Pharaoh, now that God has shown you what God can do, now will you let us go?

Pharaoh: No, no, no. Everything is okay now. And that happened without your God. It must have been my gods who changed the blood back into water, so I must be making the right decision not to let you go.

51

Frogs were all over.

Moses: Beware of what will happen now. God will not let you keep our people as slaves. You will have to let us go because your people will suffer. You are their king, so you don't want that to happen, do you?

All:
Song: "Plagues" verse 2 (Frogs)
(To the tune of: "She'll be Coming 'Round the Mountain")

**Slimy frogs will be all over everything
(croak, croak)
Slimy frogs will be all over everything
(croak, croak)
They will jump all over you-ou.
They will jump into your shoe-oe.
Slimy frogs will be all over everything.
(croak, croak)**

Pharaoh: Get these frogs out of here. Tell Moses I'll let his people go if he gets these awful frogs out of here. Oh, no, there's one under my throne, and one on my crown.

All:
Song: "It Made them Mad"
(To the tune of: "Clementine")

**Every time bad things got started
He would almost let them go;
But as soon as things got better,
He would switch and tell them NO!** *(shout No)*

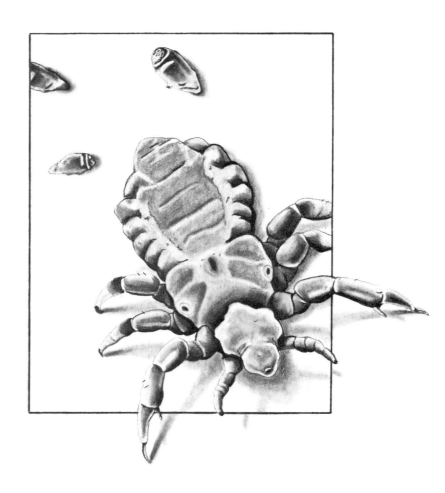

Lice itched.

Moses: Aaron, he has to see that it will hurt him if he doesn't let us go.

Aaron: Pharaoh, now are you ready to let my people go?

Pharaoh: No. I already told you. I will not let you leave. The frogs are gone now. Maybe it was my gods that made them go away, and not your God.

All:

Song: "Plagues" verse 3 (Lice)
(To the tune of: "She'll be Coming 'Round the Mountain")

Lice will make your big heads itch and itch
   and itch (scratch, scratch)
Lice will make your big heads itch and itch
   and itch (scratch, scratch)
The heads of poor and rich,
Even animals will itch
When lice make your big heads itch and itch
   and itch. (scratch, scratch)

Pharaoh: My magicians tell me that the Egyptian gods can't make these horrible lice go away. I'll have to get this Moses to get rid of them.

All:

Song: "It Made them Mad"
(To the tune of: "Clementine")

Every time bad things got started
He would almost let them go;
But as soon as things got better,
He would switch and tell them NO!

Wild animals attacked.

Moses: Our people understand that these kinds of spectacular things are signs that our God is powerful. Why doesn't Pharaoh? Maybe he will this time.

Aaron: Let my people go.

Pharaoh: No. The lice are gone. Your God is just making me madder. No. No. No. No.

All:

Song: "Plagues" verse 4 (Wild Animals)
(To be tune of: "She'll be Coming 'Round the Mountain")

**Wild animals will scare you all to death
(roar, roar)
Wild animals will scare you all to death
(roar, roar)
You'll be scared of their roars
As they bite and scratch your doors.
Wild animals will scare you all to death.
(roar, roar)**

Pharaoh: Tell Moses to get these wild animals out of Egypt. Right NOW!!!

All: **Song: "It Made them Mad"**
(To the tune of: "Clementine")

**Every time bad things got started
He would almost let them go;
But as soon as things got better,
He would switch and tell them NO!**

Narrator: Are you getting the idea that Moses and Aaron kept thinking their God had just hit Pharaoh where it would hurt? But the Pharaoh was the king and he would not let them go.

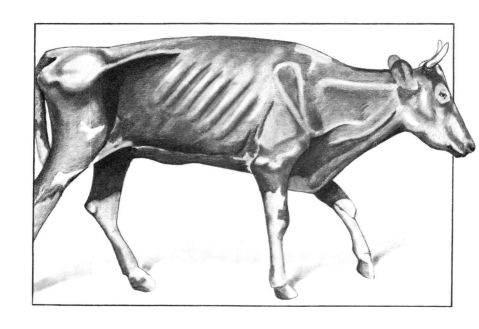

Cattle got sick and died.

Narrator: Do you think Moses gave up? No, he and Aaron went back to Pharaoh. It happened over and over and over again, with some awfully miserable kinds of bad things. Moses and Aaron gave Pharaoh reasons. Pharaoh said, "No," "Forget it," or "No, I'm king and my gods are powerful." He would be upset when the bad things happened— for a while anyway.

If the bad things had happened to everyone, Jews and Egyptians alike, it would have taken a much longer time to convince Pharaoh. But God made the bad things happen only to the Egyptians. It made the Egyptians feel all their troubles were because of the God Moses talked about and not because of something that would have happened naturally.

Moses: Let my people go, Pharaoh.

Pharaoh: No, no, no.

All:

Song: "Plagues" verse 5 (Cattle)
(To the tune of: "She'll be Coming 'Round the Mountain")

Your cattle will get sick and die like flies
  (No moos)
Your cattle will get sick and die like flies
  (No moos)
No milk will fill your cup;
No meat on which to sup
When your cattle get all sick and die like flies.
  (No moos)

All:

Song: "It Made them Mad"
(To the tune of: "Clementine")

Every time bad things got started
He would almost let them go;
But as soon as things got better;
He would switch and tell them NO !

59

Boils hurt.

All:

Song: "Plagues" verse 6 (Boils)
(To the tune of: "She'll be Coming 'Round the Mountain")

Your skin will get big sores all over it (ow,ow)
Your skin will get big sores all over it (ow, ow)
You will cry because they hurt you;
No medicine will cure you,
And you'll even get the sores down where you sit!
(ow,ow)

Pharaoh: Get rid of these boils. I can't even sit down. That isn't good for kings.

All:

Song: "It Made them Mad"
(To the tune of: "Clementine")

Every time bad things got started
He would almost let them go;
But as soon as things got better,
He would switch and tell them NO !

Hail fell from the sky.

All:

Song: "Plagues" verse 7 (Hail)
(To the tune of: "She'll be Coming 'Round the Mountain")

Icy hail will fall down on you from the sky
(knock, knock) *[Knock on the table]*
Icy hail will fall down on you from the sky
(knock, knock)
You may try to hide your head;
You may crawl beneath your bed,
But all the outside plants will surely die.
(knock, knock)

Pharaoh: I'm hiding! *[Hide the puppet underneath an arm, behind your back, or underneath the table, etc.]* Please, someone, go tell Moses I'll let them go if he'll just get rid of all this hail.

All:

Song: "It Made them Mad"
(To the tune of: "Clementine")

Every time bad things got started
He would almost let them go
But as soon as things got better
He would switch and tell them NO !

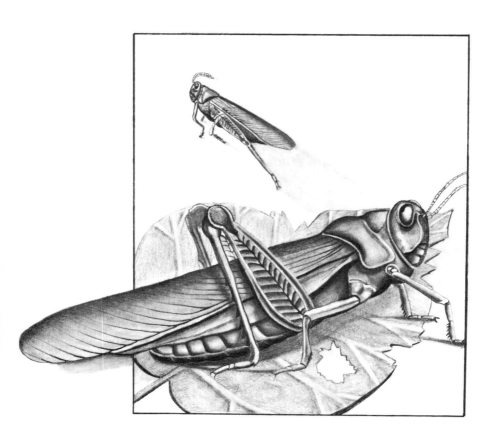

Locusts ate every plant in sight.

Aaron: We are back. How long will you not understand how great God is and let us go?

Pharaoh: Well, whom do you want to go?

Moses and Aaron: Every man, woman and child. Everyone.

Pharaoh: No. If just the men were to go, I might say OK, because if just the men went, I know they'd come back to their families. But you must be up to mischief if you want everyone to go.

All:

Song: "Plagues" verse 8 (Locusts)
(To the tune of: "She'll be Coming 'Round the Mountain")

Locust bugs will swarm all around your land
    (buzz, buzz)
Locust bugs will swarm all around your land
    (buzz, buzz)
They will eat all plants of gree-een;
No broccoli will be see-een,
When the locust bugs swarm all around your land.
    (buzz, buzz)

Pharaoh: Get rid of these bugs. Right now. They're driving me crazy. I'll do anything to get rid of them.

All:

Song: "It Made them Mad"
(To the tune of: "Clementine")

Every time bad things got started
He would almost let them go;
But as soon as things got better,
He would switch and tell them NO!

Darkness swept over the world.

Moses: I am back again to ask you to let my people go.

Pharaoh: No, never. Everything is all right now.

All:

Song: "Plagues" verse 9 (Darkness)
(To the tune of: "She'll be Coming 'Round the Mountain")

The day will turn as black as night can be.
The day will turn as black as night can be.
You won't see any faces
Or the old familiar places
When the day turns black as night could ever be.

Song: "It Made Them Mad"
(To the tune of: "Clementine")

Every time bad things got started
He would almost let them go,
But as soon as things got better,
He would switch and tell them NO!

Pharaoh: My people are scared. Moses and Aaron must stop this.

Moses and
Aaron: Let us go now and take all our things.

Pharaoh: I was thinking of letting you go— but not with all your things. No, on second thought, I will never let you go. Everything is all right, and your God can't do anything more to us.

"Let my people go!"

All:
Song: "Plagues" verse 10 (Death of the first born sons)
(To the tune of: "She'll Be Coming 'Round the Mountain")

God will give you this last chance to let us go;
God will give you this last chance to let us go.
As midnight passes by-y,
All your firstborn sons will die-ie;
And your people will cry out if we can't go.

Moses: God told me to tell you that God will kill the firstborn in every Egyptian house tonight because you, Pharaoh, have been killing the Jews which are like God's firstborn.

Narrator: God was powerful, but God was also sad when the Egyptians were suffering from the 10 bad plagues. The Egyptians were human beings, too. As we say the name of each plague, take a little drop of your wine or grape juice with your finger and put it on your plate. We will take some of the sweetness out of our own glasses to show that we care when people are upset or hurt, too.

All: Blood
Frogs
Lice
Wild animals
Cattle sickness
Boils
Hail
Locusts
Darkness
Death of the first born son

"Mark your houses with the blood of a lamb, so that God knows which are the houses of Jews."

Moses: My people, you must roast a lamb and finish eating the whole thing tonight. Then mark your houses with that lamb's blood, so God knows which are the houses of Jews.

LAMB SHANK BONE OR PASCAL LAMB

Narrator: There is a lamb bone on the Seder plate tonight, too, to remind us of that night when the Jews protected their houses with the lamb; so that God would not think it was an Egyptian house where the first born sons were killed. Can you all see this lamb shank bone that has been roasted and is on our Seder plate? *[Show it]*

Pharaoh heard the wailing of his people as the first-born Egyptian males started dying.

Pharaoh: The first born sons are starting to die in all my people's houses. This is awful! No matter how I try to cover up my ears, I can hear all the mothers and fathers crying. Oh, no! In this palace, I am the first born. What if it really was their powerful God that undid the bad things, and not my gods? I'd better call for help from Moses and Aaron before I die, too. After all, I don't want my own son to die, either.

All:

Song: "Pharaoh's Lament"
(To the tune of: "Itsy-Bitsy Spider")

My river and my sun gods have always helped me rule.
Down came the plagues, and folks think I'm a fool.
Up comes the slaves' God and tells me what to do.
I'm a roughy-toughy Pharaoh. Why won't my gods come through?

"Get out of Egypt...Take your stuff and go away."

All:

Song: "It Made Them Mad"
(To the tune of: "Clementine")

When the tenth plague scared old Pharaoh,
He'd no longer let them stay.
"Get out of Egypt," he fin'lly shouted.
"Take your stuff and go away."

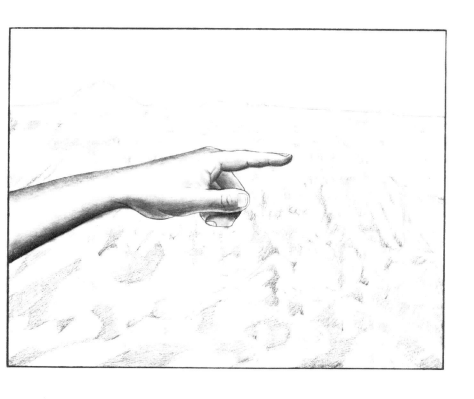

Pharaoh: Leave now. Get out of here quickly before we all die. Go worship your God. Take everything. And one, last thing (it couldn't hurt you know) will you bless me with your God's blessing this time?

"We are free!"

Moses: Yay!! We did it. We are free!

All: *[Cheer]*

MATZAH

Moses: Let's go quickly before he changes his mind.
Everyone grab your stuff. Don't bother even
baking your bread. Just grab the dough and don't
even let it rise. Just come. Everyone, pick up a
matzah in your napkin and follow us. *[As in the
Sephardic tradition, everyone at the table packs a
piece of matzah in a napkin and follows Moses. Walk
around the house saying things about the desert,
about packing so quickly, about how hard things are,
etc.]*
[Return to your places at the table.]

Matzah

Moses: Even though we don't have very much food, we do have this wonderful matzah. Let us thank God that we have this to keep us alive here in the wilderness.

All: בָּרוּךְ אַתָּה יְיָ אֱלֹהֵינוּ מֶלֶךְ הָעוֹלָם אֲשֶׁר קִדְּשָׁנוּ בְּמִצְוֹתָיו וְצִוָּנוּ עַל אֲכִילַת מַצָּה.

Baruch Atah Adonai, Eloheinu Melech ha'olam, asher kidshanu bemitzvotav vetzivanu al achilat matzah.

We praise you, Oh God, Ruler of the Universe, who makes our lives holy through commandments and who has commanded us to eat matzah to remember how quickly we had to leave Egypt.

בָּרוּךְ אַתָּה יְיָ אֱלֹהֵינוּ מֶלֶךְ הָעוֹלָם הַמּוֹצִיא לֶחֶם מִן הָאָרֶץ.

Baruch Atah Adonai, Eloheinu Melech ha'olam, hamotzi lehem min ha'aretz.
Blessed are You, Our God, Ruler of the Universe, who brings forth bread from the earth.

Taskmaster: *[to Miriam]* Here, let me help you. We're so tired of the bad things that have been happening. I'm glad Pharaoh finally let you go. Maybe it will help. I didn't want me or my son to die.

"Walk in. Believe me, our God will help us. But hurry!"

Pharaoh: The firstborns stopped dying. I'm probably safe now, too. Oh, oh! The slaves have left—now what have we done? I don't have anyone to do my work. Let's go bring them back.
Go after the Jews, the slaves! Get your chariots and horses and take all your weapons. I know the Jews left last night— but they are walking and we will have horses.

All: *[Slap legs to make the sound of running horses during the "chase".]*

Moses: That was smart of us to go before the plague was over. We should have done that a long time ago. Our God is surely great to give us light at night so we could keep going day and night to get out of there. Oh, oh, I think I see the Egyptians coming. Do you see all the dust from their horses over there? The plague must be over. They are really coming fast and are going to catch up to us. I see the Red Sea right ahead of us, and the Egyptians are behind us. There is no place for us to go. Now what are we to do? I'm no general, but I know we don't have any weapons and we don't have anywhere safe to go.

Narrator: God said to Moses, "Lift up your stick. Stretch your hand out over the sea and tell the people to walk in."

Moses: Walk in. Believe me, our God will help us. But hurry!

81

Miriam led the dancing by the shores of the Red Sea.

SECOND CUP OF WINE

Narrator: Let's taste the sweetness of almost being free—
and that does taste very sweet indeed.

בָּרוּךְ אַתָּה יְיָ אֱלֹהֵינוּ מֶלֶךְ הָעוֹלָם
בּוֹרֵא פְּרִי הַגָּפֶן.

**Baruch Atah Adonai, Eloheinu Melech
ha'olam, borei peri hagafen.**

We praise you, Oh God, Ruler of the Universe,
who creates the fruit of the vine.

Narrator: Moses lifted his stick and stretched his hand over
the sea after the children of Israel walked in.
You'll never guess what happened next, and just
in the nick of time, too. The sea divided! There
were two walls of water, and dry land was like a
road, in between them. The Jews walked on that
road through the water to the other side of the
sea. But the Egyptians were catching up and
were right behind them. When the Egyptians
were on the road in the middle of the sea, Moses
raised his hand again. The walls of water fell
down and the water rushed together again. All
the Egyptians were covered with the water and
drowned. *[Put Pharaoh into a folded napkin, or
hide him under the table]* But the Jews were free
at last. Free to be Jews.

All: Dayenu. There were plenty of blessings.

Miriam: Come on every one, let's all get up and dance.
This is something to celebrate. Let's sing to God.
*[A simple dance is to all hold hands around the
table.]*

Narrator: While we dance, let's all sing a song that thanks
God for all the things God did to free the Jews
and take care of them. "Dayenu" means, "It
would have been enough."

DAYENU

I - lu ho-tzi ho - tzi - a - nu, ho - tzi - a - nu mi - mitz - ra - yim,

ho - tzi - a - nu mi - mitz - ra - yim da - yei - nu.

(Chorus) Da - da - yei - nu,_____ da - da - yei-nu,_____ da - da - yei - nu, da -

1.,2.

3.

yei - nu da - yei - nu da - yei - nu. yei - nu da - yei - nu.

2. I-lu na-tan, na-tan la-nu, na-tan la-nu et ha-sha-bat, na-tan la-nu
et ha-sha-bat, dayeinu. (Chorus).

3. I-lu na-tan, na-tan la-nu, na-tan la-nu et ha-to-rah, na-tan la-nu et
ha-to-rah, dayeinu. (Chorus.)

Had He brought us out of Egypt
Had He brought us out of Egypt
Brought us from Egyptian bondage
Dayenu.

Had He given us the Sabbath
Had He given us the Sabbath
Given us a day for worship
Dayenu.

Had He given us the Torah
Had He given us the Torah
Given us His law to guide us,
Dayenu.

Narrator: The Jews were thankful to God for many things when they had crossed the Red Sea. They were glad they were no longer slaves and could be free. They were glad they were free to serve God. We can be thankful, too, for things that have happened to us just this past year, since our last Seder. Let's everyone think of one thing and we'll go around the table and add to our long list on this Seder night of things to be especially thankful for. *[Go around table; or have parents and children tell each other.]*

Egg

EGG

Narrator: There is still an egg on the plate in front of you. It is the symbol of freedom, and a new beginning. Can you tell us why an egg means a new beginning? *[Let people give answers.]*

Go ahead and eat your egg.

CUP OF ELIJAH

[You may prefer to wait until after the meal to read this section and the section on the Third cup of wine which follows. If you do, insert the following sections after the Grace After the Meal on page 94.]

Narrator: There is one more important guest we were hoping would come. Do you know who? We've even left a special cup of wine for this missing guest. His name is Elijah. He was a very kind teacher who lived a long time ago. He always helped those who needed it and Jews loved him for it. Jews have always thought that he would be the one who would be sent by God to tell us the world would finally be perfect—that there would be no more war, that parents would love their children and children would love their parents, and everyone would get along. Some people think that if you leave some wine out especially for Elijah, he just might come to your Seder or might come with his message a little earlier than he had planned. Some people say you can tell if he comes to your Seder to wish you a year of peace by looking to see if the wine has gone down in his cup. Do you think it has? We'll keep watching it. Maybe tonight—just maybe—when we go to open our door to let him in, he'll be there. If he is there, we would want to sing the very beautiful song Jews have just for Elijah so he'll know we are ready and he is welcome. It goes like this. Sing it with me.

Maybe tonight Elijah will come to our Seder.

EILIYAHU HANAVI

Ei - li - ya - hu   ha - na - vi,   ei - li - ya - hu   ha - tish - bi,

ei - li - ya - hu,   ei - li - ya - hu,   ei - li - ya - hu   ha - gi- la - di.

Bim - hei - ra   v' - ya- mei- nu,   ya - vo   ei - lei   -   nu

im   ma - shi - aḥ   ben   da - vid,   im   ma - shi - aḥ   ben   da - vid.

Elijah, the Prophet
Elijah, man of Tish
Elijah, Elijah
Elijah of Gilead.

Speedily, and in our time
He'll come to us,
With Messiah, son of David,
With Messiah, son of David.

Narrator: Now we are ready to go see if the guest we hope will come is here. Remember, he may not look as you thought he should. He might even come disguised. Who would like to go (with me) to open the door?
[Go to the door and open it.]

All: We all hope all Jews will be free like us to celebrate Passover and all of the Jewish holidays. We hope and pray that the world will improve for all people; that there will be peace and harmony; and that the hearts of the parents will be turned to the children and the hearts of the children to the parents. If Elijah doesn't come this year, we will keep on hoping and we will keep on working to make ours a better world.
[Close the door.]

89

The Jews were finally on their way.

THIRD CUP OF WINE

[For those reading the cup of Elijah after the meal, skip this next paragrah and the blessing following it until then and insert on page 94 after the Cup of Elijah.]

Narrator: We are happy that we are free, so it is time to drink some more wine. We know that being free doesn't get us everything, but it does give us a chance to try to do the things we want to, to make new beginnings.

All: בָּרוּךְ אַתָּה יְיָ אֱלֹהֵינוּ מֶלֶךְ הָעוֹלָם בּוֹרֵא פְּרִי הַגָּפֶן.

Baruch Atah Adonai, Eloheinu Melech ha'olam, borei peri hagafen.

We praise you, Oh God, Ruler of the Universe, who creates the fruit of the vine.

Narrator: The rest of story of Moses is a lot longer than we can tell tonight. In the next part of the story Moses will take us through the desert to get the Torah on Mt. Sinai. It is a long and exciting journey.

All:

Song: "It Made them Mad"
(To the tune of:"Clementine")

With their cattle and their matzah
Jews were fin'lly on their way.
Through the Red Sea and hot Sinai
To their own God they could pray.

91

Hand washing

AFIKOMEN OR MIDDLE MATZAH

Narrator: Before we eat our Seder meal, we break the middle matzah and put half away for our dessert. Just as the Jews with Moses could not get through the wilderness without the matzah they brought with them, we won't be able to finish our Seder without this half of the middle matzah, the *afikomen.*

We break it in two and put one part away for our dessert after we eat our Seder meal.

Please, I don't want anyone to take this *afikomen* while we are eating our dinner because we can't finish our Seder without it. If someone takes it, I will have to find it.

or

Watch this carefully. If it is gone, you will have to find it.

HAND WASHING

Narrator: It is a custom to get ready to eat by washing our hands in a special way for the Seder.

All: בָּרוּךְ אַתָּה יְיָ אֱלֹהֵינוּ מֶלֶךְ הָעוֹלָם אֲשֶׁר קִדְּשָׁנוּ בְּמִצְוֹתָיו וְצִוָּנוּ עַל נְטִילַת יָדָיִם.

Baruch Atah Adonai, Eloheinu Melech ha'olam, asher kideshanu bemizvotav vezivanu al netilat yadayim.

Blessed are You, Lord Our God, Ruler of the Universe, Who dignifies us with the commandment to wash our hands.

[Let the children take a bowl, a pitcher and a towel around the table so everyone has a chance to rinse his or her hands.]

Narrator: Now it is time for us all to enjoy our meal and appreciate those who made it for us.

SERVE THE MEAL

AFTER THE MEAL

[Look for the afikomen. It is traditional to reward those children who find it, if the children look; or to reward all the children, if the adults look.]
[For those reading the Cup of Elijah and Third cup of Wine, insert them here from page 87 to mid 91.]

GRACE AFTER THE MEAL

Narrator: We need to break the *afikomen* into pieces and give one piece to each person for dessert; so that matzah is the last food we eat at the Seder. That way we will remember all year how important freedom is, how hard it is to keep it, and how hard it is to get it back once you have lost it.

We thank God for giving us all the food we have eaten.

All: בָּרוּךְ אַתָּה יְיָ אֱלֹהֵינוּ מֶלֶךְ הָעוֹלָם, הַזָּן אֶת־הָעוֹלָם כֻּלּוֹ בְּטוּבוֹ, בְּחֵן בְּחֶסֶד וּבְרַחֲמִים.

Baruch Atah Adonai, Eloheinu Melech ha'olam, hazan et haolam kulo be tuvo behein behesed uv'rahemim.

Blessed are You, Lord Our God, Ruler of the Universe, who provides for all living things with goodness and kindness.

FOURTH CUP OF WINE

Narrator: Not all the people in the world are free yet.
[Please insert your own prayers or comments here for those who are not yet free.] The fourth cup of wine is full of the sweetness we hope for the world. We hope the world will soon be full of peace and that the people of the world will be happy, free, and loved. May all be free as we are tonight to serve You.

בָּרוּךְ אַתָּה יְיָ אֱלֹהֵינוּ מֶלֶךְ הָעוֹלָם בּוֹרֵא פְּרִי הַגָּפֶן.

All: Baruch Atah Adonai, Eloheinu Melech ha'olam, borei peri hagafen.
Blessed is the Lord Our God who created the fruit of the vine.

All: For us and all Israel
For us and all people everywhere
Next year in Jerusalem
Next year a year of peace
Next year every one free, and loved.

לְשָׁנָה הַבָּאָה בִּירוּשָׁלָיִם.

Le Shanah habaah bi rushalayim.
Next year in Jerusalem

OPTIONAL FOUR QUESTIONS

[There may be an older child in the group who would like the honor of reciting the Four Questions. If so, insert here and see if the rest of the children can answer them. Alternatively, insert them at the beginning.]

Child:

מַה נִּשְׁתַּנָּה הַלַּיְלָה הַזֶּה מִכָּל הַלֵּילוֹת.

Ma nish-ta-na ha-lai-lah ha-zeh mi-kol ha-lei lot?
Why is this night different from all other nights?

שֶׁבְּכָל הַלֵּילוֹת אָנוּ אוֹכְלִין חָמֵץ וּמַצָּה, הַלַּיְלָה הַזֶּה כֻּלּוֹ מַצָּה.

She-b'-hol ha-lei-lot a-nu oh-lin-ha'metz u-ma-tzah. Ha-lai-lah ha-zeh, ku-lo matzah.
On all other nights, we eat either leavened bread or matzah; on this night—only matzah.

שֶׁבְּכָל הַלֵּילוֹת אָנוּ אוֹכְלִין שְׁאָר יְרָקוֹת, הַלַּיְלָה הַזֶּה מָרוֹר.

She-b'-hol ha-lei lot a-nu oh-lin sh'-ar y'-ra-kot. Ha-lei-lah ha-zeh, maror.
On all other nights, we eat all kinds of herbs; on this night, we especially eat bitter herbs.

שֶׁבְּכָל הַלֵּילוֹת אֵין אָנוּ מַטְבִּילִין
אֲפִילוּ פַּעַם אֶחָת, הַלַּיְלָה הַזֶּה
שְׁתֵּי פְעָמִים.

**She-be-hol ha-lei-lot ein a-nu mat-bi-lin a-fi-lu
pa-am e-hat. Ha-lai-lah ha-zeh, sh-tai-pi-ah-
mim.**

On all other nights, we do not dip herbs at all; on
this night we dip them twice.

שֶׁבְּכָל הַלֵּילוֹת אָנוּ אוֹכְלִין בֵּין
יוֹשְׁבִין וּבֵין מְסֻבִּין, הַלַּיְלָה הַזֶּה
כֻּלָּנוּ מְסֻבִּין.

**She-bi-hul ha-lei-lot a-nu och-lin bein yosh-vin
oo-vein mis-oo-been. Ha-lai-lah hazeh, ku-la-
nu m'-su-bin.**

On all other nights, we eat in an ordinary manner;
tonight we dine with special ceremony.

SONGS

PHARAOH DOESN'T PAY

(To the tune of: "I've Been Working on the Railroad")
I've been working on these buildings;
Pharaoh doesn't pay.
I've been doing what he tells me
Like making bricks from clay.
Can't you hear the master calling,
"Hurry up, make a brick!"
Can't you feel the master hurt me
Until I'm feeling sick.
Oh is this a mess,
Oh is this a mess,
Oh is this a mess, for Jews, for Jews.
Oh is this a mess,
Oh is this a mess,
Oh is this a mess for Jews.
Someone's in the palace with Pharaoh —
Someone's in the palace we know, ow, ow, ow,
Someone's in the palace with Pharaoh —
Does he know they treat us so?
Keep singing work, work, work all day,
Work all day and then some mo – ore,
Work, work, work all day —
Does he know they treat us so?

IT MADE THEM MAD
NO, NO, NO, NO
(To the tune of: "Clementine")

It made them mad to hear the answer
Pharaoh would not let them go.
God would help them, with a signal.
Mighty power God would show.

No, no, no, no, no, no, no, no,
That was all that Pharaoh said.
With no way to beat his army,
They would change his mind instead.

Every time bad things got started
He would almost let them go;
But as soon as things got better,
He would switch and tell them NO! *(shout no)*

When the tenth plague scared old Pharaoh,
He'd no longer let them stay.
"Get out of Egypt,"he fin'lly shouted.
"Take your stuff and go away."

With their cattle and some matzah
Jews were fin'lly on their way.
Through the Red Sea and hot Sinai
To their own God they could pray.

BAD THINGS WILL COME TO EGYPT: THE PLAGUES

(To the tune of: "She'll be Coming 'Round the Mountain")

Bad things will come to Egypt, don't you know
Bad things will come to Egypt, don't you know
Bad things will come to Egypt,
Bad things will come to Egypt,
Bad things will come to Egypt till we go.

First, God will change the water into blood (ick, ick)
First God will change the water into blood (ick, ick)
There'll be nothing left to drink;
With no baths you all will stink
When God changes all the water into blood. (ick, ick)

Slimy frogs will be all over everything (croak, croak)
Slimy frogs will be all over everything (croak, croak)
They will jump all over you-ou.
They will jump into your shoe-oe.
Slimy frogs will be all over everything. (croak, croak)

Lice will make your big heads itch and itch and itch
    (scratch, scratch)
Lice will make your big heads itch and itch and itch
    (scratch, scratch)
The heads of poor and rich,
Even animals will itch
When lice make your big heads itch and itch and itch.
    (scratch, scratch)

Wild animals will scare you all to death (roar, roar)
Wild animals will scare you all to death (roar, roar)
You'll be scared of their roars
As they bite and scratch your doors.
Wild animals will scare you all to death. (roar, roar)

Your cattle will get sick and die like flies (no moos)
Your cattle will get sick and die like flies (no moos)
No milk will fill your cup;
No meat on which to sup
When your cattle get all sick and die like flies. (no moos)

Your skin will get big sores all over it (ow, ow)
Your skin will get big sores all over it (ow, ow)
You will cry 'cause they hurt you;
No medicine will cure you,
And you'll even get the sores down where you sit. (ow, ow)

Icy hail will fall down on you from the sky
   (knock, knock)*(knock on the table)*
Icy hail will fall down on you from the sky (knock, knock)
You may try to hide your head;
You may crawl beneath your bed,
But all the outside plants will surely die. (knock, knock)

Locust bugs will swarm all round your land (buzz, buzz)
Locust bugs will swarm all round your land (buzz, buzz)
They will eat all plants of gre-en;
No broccoli will be se-en
When the locust bugs swarm all around your land.
   (buzz, buzz)

The day will turn as black as night can be.
The day will turn as black as night can be.
You won't see any faces
And the old familiar places
When the day turns black as night could ever be.

God will give you this last chance to let us go;
God will give you this last chance to let us go.
As midnight passes by-y,
All your firstborn sons will die-ie;
And your people will cry out if we can't go.

Bad things will come to Egypt, don't you know
Bad things will come to Egypt, don't you know
Bad things will come to Egypt,
Bad things will come to Egypt,
Bad things will come to Egypt, till we go.

PHARAOH'S LAMENT

(To the tune of: "The Itsy-bitsy Spider")

My river and my sun gods have always helped me rule.
Down came the plagues and folks think I'm a fool.
Up comes the slaves' God and tells me what to do.
I'm a roughy-toughy Pharaoh. Why won't my gods come
   through?

HAD GADYA (AN ONLY KID)

Refrain

Ḥad gad - ya,_____ ḥad gad - ya 1. di -

z' - van a - bah bit - rei__ zu - zei. 2. V' - a - tah shun - rah
3. V' - a - tah kal - bah

v' - a - ḥal l' - gad - ya. (. . . . .) Di - z' - van a - bah
v' - na - shaḥ l' - shun - rah d' - a - ḥal l' - gad - ya.

bit - rei__ zu - zei. 4. V' - a - tah ḥu -trah v'hi-kah l'-kal - bah d' -

no - shaḥ l' - shun - rah d' - a - ḥal l' - gad -

ya di - z' - van a - bah bit - rei __ zu - zei.

5. V'-a-tah nu-rah v'sa-raf l'ḥu-trah.
d'hi-kah l'ḥal-bah d'na-shaḥ l'shun-rah,
d'a-ḥal l'gad-ya di-z'van a-bah bit-rei zuzei . . .

6. V'-a-tah ma-yah v'ḥa-vah l'nu-rah,
d'sa-raf l'ḥu-trah d'hi-kah l'ḥal-bah,
d'na-shaḥ l'shun-rah d'a-ḥal l'gad-ya
di-z'van a-bah bit-rei zuzei . . .

7. V'-a-tah to-rah v'sha-tah l'ma-yah,
d'ḥa-vah l'nu-rah d'sa-raf l'ḥu-trah,
d'hi-kah l'ḥal-bah d'na-shaḥ l'shun-rah,
d'a-ḥal l'gad-ya di-z'van a-bah bit-rei zuzei . . .

8. V'-a-tah ha-sho-ḥeit v'sha-ḥat l'to-rah,
d'sha-tah l'ma-yah d'ḥa-vah l'nu-rah,
d'sa-raf l'ḥu-trah, d'hi-kah l'ḥal-bah,
d'na-shaḥ l'shun-rah d'a-ḥal l'gad-ya,
di-z'van a-bah bit-rei zuzei . . .

9. V'-a-tah mal-aḥ ha-ma-vet v'sha-ḥat la-sho-ḥeit,
d'sha-ḥat l'to-rah d'sha-tah l'ma-yah,
d'ḥa-vah l'nu-rah d'sa-raf l'ḥu-trah,
d'hi-kah l'ḥal-bah d'na-shaḥ l'shun-rah,
d'a-ḥal l'gad-ya di-z'van a-bah bit-rei zuzei . . .

102

An Only Kid, an Only Kid

Chorus: That my father bought for two zuzim Had Gadya

1 Then came the cat
And ate the kid

Chorus

2 Then came the dog
And bit the cat
That ate the kid

Chorus

3 Then came the stick
And beat the dog
That bit the cat
That ate the kid

Chorus

4 Then came the fire
And burned the stick
That beat the dog
That bit the cat
That ate the kid

Chorus

5 Then came the water
And quenched the fire
That burned the stick
That beat the dog
That bit the cat
That ate the kid

Chorus

6 Then came the ox
And drank the water
That quenched the fire
That burned the stick
That beat the dog
That bit the cat
That ate the kid

Chorus

7 Then came the butcher
And killed the ox
That drank the water
That quenched the fire
That burned the stick
That beat the dog
That bit the cat
That ate the kid

Chorus

8 Then came the angel of death
And slew the butcher
That killed the ox
That drank the water
That quenched the fire
That burned the stick
That beat the dog
That bit the cat
That ate the kid

Chorus

9 Then came the Holy One, blessed be He,
And destroyed the angel of death
That slew the butcher
That killed the ox
That drank the water
That quenched the fire
That burned the stick
That beat the dog
That bit the cat
That ate the kid

Chorus

EHAD MI YODEAH (WHO KNOWS ONE)

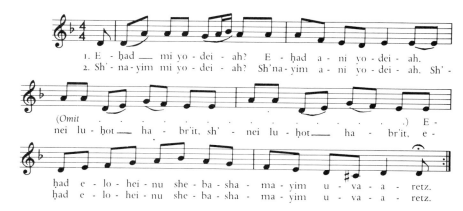

1. E - ḥad —— mi yo - dei - ah? E - ḥad a - ni yo - dei - ah.
2. Sh' - na - yim mi yo - dei - ah? Sh'na - yim a - ni yo - dei - ah. Sh' -

(Omit   .) E -
nei lu - ḥot —— ha - br'it, sh' - nei lu - ḥot —— ha - br'it, e -

ḥad e - lo - hei - nu she - ba - sha - ma - yim u - va - a - retz.
ḥad e - lo - hei - nu she - ba - sha - ma - yim u - va - a - retz.

3. Sh'-lo-sha mi yo-dei-ah? Sh'-lo-sha a-ni yo-dei-ah.
   Sh'lo-sha a-vot. Sh'nei . . . (etc.)

4. Ar'-bah mi yo-dei-ah? Ar'-bah a-ni yo-dei-ah.
   Ar'-bah i-ma-hot. Sh'-lo-sha . . .

5. Ḥa-mi-sha mi yo-dei-ah? Ḥa-mi-sha a-ni yo-dei-ah.
   Ḥa-mi-sha ḥum-shei to-rah. Ar'-bah . . .

6. Shi-sha mi yo-dei-ah? Shi-sha a-ni yo-dei-ah.
   Shi-sha sid-rei mish-na. Ḥa-mi-sha . . .

7. Shi-va mi yo-dei-ah? Shi-va a-ni yo-dei-ah.
   Shi-va y'mei shab-ta. Shi-sha . . .

8. Sh'mo-na mi yo-dei-ah? Sh'mo-na a-ni yo-dei-ah.
   Sh'mo-na y'-mei mi-lah. Shi-va . . .

9. Ti-sha mi yo-dei-ah? Ti-sha a-ni yo-dei-ah.
   Ti-sha yar-ḥei lei-dah. Sh'mo-na . . .

10. A-sa-rah mi yo-dei-ah? A-sa-rah a-ni yo-dei-ah.
    A-sa-rah dib'ra-yah. Ti-sha . . .

11. A-ḥad a-sar mi yo-dei-ah? A-ḥad a-sar a-ni yo-dei-ah.
    A-ḥad a-sar koh-va-yah. A-sa-rah . . .

12. Sh'-neim a-sar mi yo-dei-ah? Sh'-neim a-sar a-ni yo-dei-ah.
    Sh'-neim a-sar shiv-ta-yah. A-ḥad a-sar . . .

13. Sh'lo-sha a-sar mi yo-dei-ah? Sh'lo-sha a-sar a-ni yo-dei-ah.
    Sh'lo-sha a-sar mi-da-yah.

WHO KNOWS ONE

1. Who knows one? I know one.
One is our God, in heaven and on earth.

2. Who knows two? I know two.
Two are the tables of the commandments;
One is our God, in heaven and on earth.

3. Who knows three? I know three.
Three is the number of the patriarchs;
Two are the tables of the commandments;
One is our God, in heaven and on earth.

4. Who knows four? I know four.
Four is the number of the matriarchs;
Three, the number of patriarchs;
Two are the tables of the commandments;
One is our God, in heaven and on earth.

5. Who knows five? I know five.
Five books there are in the Torah;
Four is the number of the matriarchs;
Three, the number of the patriarchs;
Two are the tables of the commandments;
One is our God, in heaven and on earth.

6. Who knows six? I know six.
Six sections the Mishnah has;
Five books there are in the Torah;
Four is the number of matriarchs;
Three, the number of the patriarchs;
Two are the tables of the commandments;
One is our God, in heaven and on earth.

7. Who knows seven? I know seven.
Seven days there are in a week;
Six sections the Mishnah has;
Five books there are in the Torah;
Four is the number of matriarchs;
Three, the number of patriarchs;
Two are the tables of the commandments;
One is our God, in heaven and on earth.

8. Who knows eight? I know eight.
Eight are the days to the service of the covenant;
Seven days there are in the week;
Six sections the Mishnah has;
Five books there are in the Torah;
Four is the number of the matriarchs;
Three, the number of the patriarchs;
Two are the tables of the commandments;
One is our God, in heaven and on earth.

9. Who knows nine? I know nine.
Nine is the number of the holidays;
Eight are the days to the service of the covenant;
Seven days there are in a week;
Six sections in the Mishnah;
Five books there are in the Torah;

Four is the number of the matriarchs;
Three, the number of the patriarchs;
Two are the tables of the commandments;
One is our God, in heaven and on earth.

10. Who knows ten? I know ten.
Ten commandments were given on Sinai;
Nine is the number of the holidays;
Eight are the days to the service of the covenant;
Seven days there are in a week;
Six sections the Mishnah has;
Five books there are in the Torah;
Four is the number of the matriarchs;
Three, the number of the patriarchs;
Two are the tables of the commandments;
One is our God, in heaven and on earth.

11. Who knows eleven? I know eleven.
Eleven were the stars in Joseph's dream;
Ten commandments were given on Sinai;
Nine is the number of the holidays;
Eight are the days to the service of the covenant;
Seven days there are in a week;
Six sections the Mishnah has;
Five books there are in the Torah;
Four is the number of matriarchs;
Three, the number of the patriarchs;
Two are the tables of the commandments;
One is our God, in heaven and on earth.

12. Who knows twelve? I know twelve.
Twelve are the tribes of Israel;
Eleven were the stars in Joseph's dream;
Ten commandments were given on Sinai;
Nine is the number of the holidays;
Eight are the days to the service of the covenant;
Seven days there are in a week;
Six sections the Mishnah has;
Five books there are in the Torah;
Four is the number of the matriarchs;
Three, the number of the patriarchs;
Two are the tables of the commandments;
One is our God, in heaven and on earth.

13. Who knows thirteen? I know thirteen.
Thirteen are the attributes of God;
Twelve are the tribes of Israel;
Eleven were the stars in Joseph's dream;
Ten commandments were given on Sinai;
Nine is the number of the holidays;
Eight are the days to the service of the covenant;
Seven days there are in a week;
Six sections the Mishnah has;
Five books there are in the Torah;
Four is the number of the matriarchs;
Three, the number of the patriarchs;
Two are the tables of the commandments;
One is our God, in heaven and on earth.

ADIR HU (GOD OF MIGHT)

(*Hebrew verses 2–4*
begin here)

1. A - dir hu   a - dir   hu   yiv -
1. God of Might,   God   of   Right,_____

neh   vei - to   b' -   ka - rov   bim - hei - rah_____
Thee   we   give   all__   glo - ry   Thine   all   praise _____

bim - hei - rah   b' - ya - mei - nu   b' - ka - rov
in   these   days   As   in   a - ges   hoa - ry,

Eil   b' - nei   eil   b' - nei   b'nei   veit - ḥa   b' - ka - rov.
When   we   hear,   year   by   year,   Free - dom's   won - drous   sto - ry.

2. Ba-ḥur hu, ga-dol hu, da-gul hu . . .
3. Na-or hu, sa-giv hu, iz-uz hu . . .
4. Po-deh hu, tsa-dik hu, ka-dosh hu . . .

2. Now as erst, when Thou first
    Mad'st the proclamation,
    Warning loud ev'ry proud,
    Ev'ry tyrant nation,
    We Thy fame still proclaim
    Bend in adoration.

3. Be with all who in thrall
    To their task are driven;
    In Thy power speed the hour
    When their chains are riven;
    Earth around will resound
    Gleeful hymns to heaven.

(An alternate text)

1. God of Might, God of Right,
    We would bow before Thee,
    Sing Thy praise in these days,
    Celebrate Thy glory,
    As we hear, year by year,
    Freedom's wond'rous story:

2. How God gave to each slave
    Promised liberation,
    This great word Pharaoh heard
    Making proclamation:
    Set them free to serve Me
    As a holy nation.

3. We enslaved thus were saved
    Through God's might appearing,
    So we pray for the day
    When we shall be hearing
    Freedom's call reaching all,
    Mankind God revering.

OTHER BOOKS ABOUT PASSOVER FOR YOUNG CHILDREN

Adler, David A., *A Picture Book of Passover*, Holiday House, New York,1982. Illustrations by Linda Heller. This book tells the story of Exodus in a very readable form.

Chaikin, Miriam, *Ask Another Question: The Story and Meaning of Passover*, Clarion Books, Ticknor & Fields: A Houghton Mifflin Company, New York, 1985. Illustrations by Marvin Friedman. A very helpful history of the holiday and Haggadah.

Chaikin, Miriam, *Exodus*, Holiday House, New York, 1987. Illustrated by Charles Mikolaycak. Adapted from the Book of Exodus, this includes not only the Passover story but the whole of the book of Exodus. Wonderful illustrations.

Hirsch, Marilyn, *I Love Passover*, Holiday House, New York, 1985. A combination of the Passover story, preparation for Seder, and the Seder told from an excited child's perspective. Children have an easy time identifying with the illustrations.

Hirsch, Marilyn, *One Little Goat, A Passover Song*, adapted and illustrated by Marilyn Hirsch, Holiday House, New York, 1979. An illustrated version of the lively, traditional Passover song, *"Had Gadya"*.

Hutton, Warwick, *Moses in the Bullrushes*, Atheneum, New York, 1986. Beautiful watercolor drawings to accompany the story of baby Moses.

Marcus, Audrey Friedman, and Raymond A. Zwerin, *But This Night is Different: A Seder Experience*, Union of American Hebrew Congregations, New York, 1980. Illustrations by Judith Gwyn Brown. What a Seder is like.

Medoff, Francine, *The Mouse in the Matzah Factory*, Kar-Ben Copies, Rockville, MD, 1983. Illustrated by David Goldstein. How matzah is made; beginning to end.

Miller, Deborah Uchill, *Only Nine Chairs: A Tall Tale for Passover*, Kar-Ben Copies, Rockville, MD, 1982. Illustrations by Karen Otrove. A rather hilarious kid's eye view of the family Seder in verse.

Rosen, Anne, Jonathan Rosen and Norma Rosen, *A Family Passover*, Jewish Publication Society of America, Philadelphia, 1980. Photographs by Laurence Salzmann. Preparations for the holiday.

RECIPES FOR CHAROSET

YEMENITES season chopped dates, figs, sesame seeds with hot chili pepper.

ISRAELI CHAROSET

2 apples, peeled and chopped
3 bananas, mashed
1/2 C peanuts, chopped
1/2 orange, juice and rind
1/2 lemon, juice and rind
1/4 C sweet red wine
2 tsp cinnamon
sugar to taste

Blend everything together.

ASHKENAZI CHAROSET

2 C apples, peeled and chopped
1 C walnuts or pecans, chopped
1/4 C sweet red wine
3 TB honey
2 tsp cinnamon

Finely chop apples and nuts together. Blend together with all other ingredients.

ITALIANS add chopped hard boiled eggs to the Ashkenazi mixture.

SEPHARDIC CHAROSET
1/2 C sliced dates, pitted
1/2 C dried apricots
2 C apples, peeled and chopped
1/2 C walnuts, chopped
1 TB sweet red wine
1 TB sugar

Combine dates, apricots and apples. Add water to cover.
Cook on low heat until tender enough to mash, at least 1/2
hour. Drain water. Mash. Add nuts, red wine and sugar. Blend
together.

GUEST LIST AND PUPPET PLAYERS

Year	19___	19___	19___	19___
Role	played by	played by	played by	played by
Moses				
Aaron				
Yocheved				
Miriam				
Slave				
Pharaoh				
Princess				
Taskmaster				
Sheep				
Narrator				
Other guests				

112

Puppet instructions

To finish the puppets

1. **Take puppets out of book** along perforations (adult help needed).
2. **Color** with pencils, crayons or markers. Add ribbons, glitter, material or sequins.
3. **Cut out** on dotted lines.
4. **To make a finger puppet** (your 2nd and 3rd fingers do the walking):
   Tape a rubber band parallel to and one inch from the bottom of the puppet. Insert your fingers so that the fingers are feet.

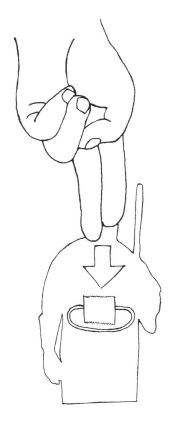

OR

To make a rod puppet: Tape the puppet to a stick (straw, pencil, chopstick, or spoon handle.)

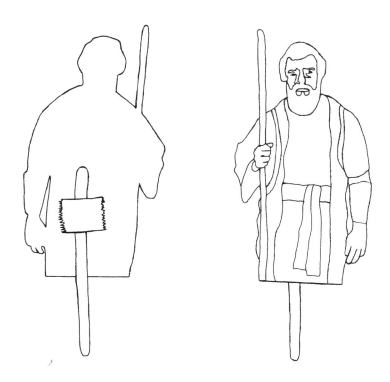

Pharaoh

Pharaoh

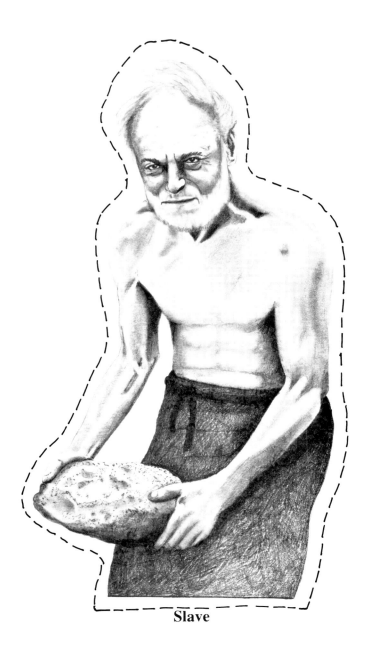

Slave

Slave

Yocheved

Yocheved

Miriam

Miriam

Princess

114-E

Princess

Taskmaster

Taskmaster

Moses

114-G

Moses

Sheep

Sheep

Aaron

Aaron

ABOUT THE AUTHOR:

Mary Ann Barrows Wark believes her major accomplishment and joy is being a mother. She received her A.B. Radcliffe College, Harvard University; M.A.T. Harvard Graduate School of Education; and J.D. Boston University School of Law. She wrote this Haggadah for her family Seder when her son was 2 years old. For the past several years, she has used it successfully at family Seders, in model Seders, with preschool groups in religious school, and at family education events. She serves as a member of the Board at Mt. Zion Hebrew Congregation. She is President of Resources for Child Caring, Inc., St. Paul and serves on the Board of the Children's Museum, St. Paul, where she has helped design exhibits. She teaches law school part-time and lives in St. Paul with her husband, David and son, Barry. Her step-children Kathleen and Jeffry are adults.

ABOUT THE ILLUSTRATOR:

Craig Oskow is a native New York artist. He received his Bachelor of Fine Arts from Otis Art Institute of Parsons School of Design in Los Angeles. He now resides in Minneapolis, Minnesota with his wife, Catherine, and son, Kevin. He is currently concentrating on Jewish art.

ABOUT THE BOOK

The main text of this Haggadah was set by Bob's Litho/Satellite Cold Type in St. Paul, Minnesota in 12 pt. Times Roman. The transliterations and English translations of the Hebrew are set in 12 pt. Helvetica. The Hebrew was set by Tova Press, Brooklyn, New York in Haddassah. The book was printed by Western Printing, Minneapolis, Minnesota on white Howard linen paper and bound in Wire-O.

Order Form

There are 9 puppet roles and you will need a minimum of 6 books. (There are no more than 6 characters per scene.)

Each copy includes a set of 9 puppets to cut-out.

RETAIL PRICE   Single copy: $11.95
                       Family set of 6 $69.95

YES, PLEASE SEND ME the following copies of WE TELL IT TO OUR CHILDREN:

Quantity		Total
	At single copy price of $11.95 ppd	
	Sets of 6 at price of $69.95 ppd	
	Subtotal	
	Shipping and handling* (see below)	
	MN RESIDENTS add 6% sales tax	
	Total	

Shipping and handling by U.S. Mail Book Rate:

Under $30.00   add $2.00
$30.01-50   add $3.00
$50.01 +   add $4.00

Name _____

Address _____

City _____ State _____ Zip _____

Telephone (_____) _____-_____

MAKE OUT CHECKS TO: "MENSCH MAKERS PRESS"

SEND TO: MENSCH MAKERS PRESS
             1588 Northrop St.
             St. Paul, MN 55108-1322

Orders shipped within 3-4 weeks.